1001 COOL BEST EVER JOKES

W9-BXZ-613

Published by Hinkler Books Pty Ltd 2020
45–55 Fairchild Street
Heatherton Victoria 3202 Australia
www.hinkler.com.au

© Hinkler Books Pty Ltd 2020

Internal illustrations: Glen Singleton
Cover illustration: Rob Kiely
Cover design: Hinkler Books Design Studio
Typeset by MPS Limited

All rights reserved. No part of this publication may be reproduced, stored in a retrieval system, or transmitted in any way or by any means, electronic, mechanical, photocopying, recording or otherwise, without the prior written permission of Hinkler Books Pty Ltd.

ISBN: 978 1 4889 4441 3

Printed and bound in Malaysia

CONTENTS

Animals

1 **W**hat is a polygon?
A dead parrot.

2 **W**hat do owls sing when it's raining?
Too wet to woo.

3 **W**here do horses live?
Neighborhoods.

4 **W**hy don't elephants
ever get rich?
*Because they work for
peanuts.*

Obviously a
very rich elephant
who chose not
to eat his
peanuts

PEANUTS   PEANUTS

5 **W**hat kind of animal goes "OOM"?
A cow walking backwards.

6 **W**hat type of snake is good at math?
An adder.

7 **W**hat was the first nursery rhyme animal in space?
The cow that jumped over the moon.

8 **W**here do penguins go to vote?
The South Poll.

9 **W**hat do alpacas worry about?
Llamageddon.

10 **W**hen do kangaroos celebrate their birthdays?
During leap years.

11 **W**hat do llamas worry about?
The Alpacalypse.

12 **W**hat do you get when you cross a porcupine and a sloth?
A slow poke.

13 **W**hat did one bee say to her nosy neighbor bee?
"Mind your own bees' nest!"

14 **W**hat do you do with a mouse that squeaks?
You oil him.

15 **W**here does a pig go to pawn his watch?
A ham hock shop.

16 **W**hat happens when a chimpanzee sprains his ankle?

He gets a monkey wrench.

17 **W**hat happened to the male bee that fell in love?

He got stuck on his honey.

18 **W**hat do you get if you cross a hyena with a bouillon cube?

A laughing stock.

19 **W**hat's the best way to catch a monkey?

Climb a tree and act like a banana.

20 **W**hat did the judge say when the skunk walked into the courtroom?

Odor in the court.

21 **W**hy do tigers have stripes?

So they're not spotted.

22 **H**ow do snails fight?

They slug it out.

23 **W**hat do you get if you cross a tiger with a sheep?
A striped sweater.

24 **W**hat do you get if you cross a tiger with a snowman?
Frostbite.

25 **W**hat do you call two birds in love?
Tweethearts.

26 **H**ow do you keep a rhino from charging?
Unplug it.

27 **W**hy should you never trust a pig with a secret?
Because it's bound to squeal.

28 **W**here do you find a dog with no legs?
Exactly where you left it.

29 **W**hat do you call a crazy chicken?

A cuckoo cluck.

30 **W**hat do you get if you cross Bambi with a ghost?

Bamboo.

31 **W**hat do you call an alligator in a vest?

An investigator!

32 **W**hat animal wears a wig?

A bald eagle!

33 **W**hat is white, lives in the Himalayas and lays eggs?

The Abominable Snow Chicken.

34 **W**hat did the firefly say to the other firefly?

You glow, girl.

35 **W**hat do you call a cow with no legs?

Ground beef!

36 **W**hat do you call a cow with two legs?

Lean meat!

37 **W**hat does a spider wear to get married?

A webbing dress.

38 **O**n which side does an eagle have most of its feathers?

On the outside.

39 **W**hat kind of haircuts do bees get?

Buzz cuts.

40 **W**hy don't you ever see elephants hiding in trees?

Because they're really good at it!

41 **W**hat do you call a crate of ducks?

A box of quackers.

42 **W**hat's the difference between a mouse and an elephant?

About a ton.

43 **W**hat do you get when you cross a centipede with a parrot?

A walkie talkie.

44 **W**hat does an evil hen lay?

Deviled eggs.

45 **W**hat happened to two frogs that caught the same bug at the same time?

They got tongue-tied.

The luckiest bug in the pond

46 **W**hat kind of key doesn't unlock any doors?

A don-key.

47 **W**hat kind of key opens a coconut?

A mon-key.

48 **W**hat do you call a fish without an eye?

Fsh.

MUM! Has the elephant been in my bedroom again?

49 **W**hat time is it when an elephant climbs into your bed?

Time to get a new bed.

50 **W**hat do you get if you pour hot water down a rabbit hole?

Hot cross bunnies.

51 **W**hat do you call bears with no ears?

B.

52 **W**hy is it hard to play cards in the jungle?

There are too many cheetahs.

53 **W**hat do you get if you cross a pig with a zebra?

Striped sausage.

54 **W**hen is it bad luck to see a black cat?

When you're a mouse.

55 **W**hat's a vulture's favorite dinner?

Leftovers.

56 **W**hy can't you trust the king of the jungle?

Because he's lion.

57 **W**hat do porcupines say when they kiss?

Ouch.

58 **W**hat do you get if you cross a duck with a firework?

A fire-quacker.

59 **W**hy do buffaloes always travel in herds?

Because they're afraid of getting mugged by elephants.

60 **W**hat do you call the autobiography of a shark?

A fishy story.

61 **H**ow do you make an octopus laugh?

With ten-tickles!

62 **H**ow does an octopus go to war?

Well armed.

The Mackerel do look nice today!

63 **W**here do sharks shop?

The fish market.

64 **W**hat do you call a traveling mosquito?

An itch hiker.

65 **W**hat is a duck's favorite T.V. show?
The feather forecast.

66 **W**hat did the rabbit give his girlfriend when they got engaged?
A 24-carrot ring.

67 **W**hat do you do if your chicken feels sick?
Give her an eggs-ray.

68 **H**ow do you get a squirrel to like you?
Act like a nut!

69 **W**hy can't Elsa walk the dog?
Because she will let it go.

70 **W**hat did the Dalmatian say after lunch?
That hit the spot!

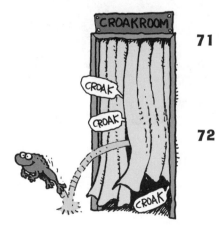

71 **W**here do tadpoles change into frogs?
The croakroom.

72 **W**hat do elephants take when they can't sleep?
Trunkquilisers.

73   **W**hy do elephants have trunks?

Because they can't fit everything into their handbags.

74   **H**ow do ducks play tennis?

With a quacket.

75   **W**hy do bears have fur coats?

Because they can't get plastic raincoats in their size!

76   **W**hat would you get if you crossed a hunting dog with a journalist?

A news hound.

77   **W**hy are elephants wrinkled?

Have you ever tried to iron one?

78 **W**hat's a crocodile's favorite game?

Snap!

79 **W**hat did one flea say to the other flea?

Shall we walk or take the dog?

80 **W**here is the hottest place in the jungle?

Under a gorilla.

81 **H**ow do you find where a flea has bitten you?

You start from scratch.

82 **W**hat do you get when you cross a porcupine and a balloon?

POP!

83 **W**hat do you call an elephant in an elevator?

Stuck.

84 **H**ow does a porcupine play leap frog?

Very, very carefully.

85 **W**hat happened when the cat swallowed a ball of yarn?

She had mittens.

86 **W**hy aren't turkeys invited to dinner?

Because they always use fowl language.

87 **W**hat do you call a bull taking a nap?

A bull dozer.

88 **W**hat is the biggest ant in the world?

An eleph-ant.

89 **W**hat's even bigger than that?

A gi-ant!

90 **H**ow many ants are needed to fill an apartment?

Ten-ants.

91 **W**here do ants eat?

A restaur-ant.

92 **W**hich sort of bird steals from banks?

A robin.

93 **W**hat bird is always out of breath?

A puffin.

94 **H**ow do fireflies start a race?

Ready, set, glow!

95 **W**hat do you get if you cross a leopard with a watchdog?

A terrified postman.

96 **W**hy were flies playing football in a saucer?
They were playing for the cup.

97 **W**hat do you call a bird that lives underground?
A mynah bird.

98 **W**hich birds steal the soap from the bath?
Robber ducks.

99 **H**ow do we know that owls are smarter than chickens?
Have you ever heard of Kentucky Fried Owl?

100 What does an octopus wear when it's cold?

A coat of arms.

101 What is a parrot's favorite game?

Hide and speak.

102 What do parrots eat?

Polyfilla.

103 **W**hat do you call a
Scottish parrot?

A Macaw.

104 **W**hat's small,
squeaks, and
hangs out in
caves?

Stalagmice.

105 **W**hat do you call a
mouse that can pick
up a monster?

Sir.

106 **W**hat happens
when ducks fly
upside-down?

They quack up.

107 How can you tell the difference between a rabbit and a monster?

Ever tried getting a monster into a rabbit hutch?

108 What do you get if you cross a parrot with a woodpecker?

A bird that talks in Morse code.

109 Now you see it, now you don't. What could you be looking at?

A black cat walking over a zebra crossing!

110 Where do Noah's bees live?

In ark hives.

111   **W**hat's another name for a clever duck?

A wise quacker!

112   **W**hat is a termite's favorite breakfast?

Oak-meal.

113   **W**hat's the difference between a mosquito and a fly?

Try zipping up a mosquito!

114   **W**hy did the insects drop the centipede from their football team?

He took too long to put on his shoes!

An owl with laryngitis

115   **W**hat happened when the owl lost his voice?

He didn't give a hoot.

116 **W**hat did the lion say to his cubs when he taught them to hunt?

Don't walk across the road until you see the zebra crossing.

117 **W**hat do lions say before they go out hunting for food?

Let us prey.

118 **W**hat does a lion brush his mane with?

A catacomb.

119 **W**hat happened when the lion ate the comedian?

He felt funny.

120 **H**ow can you get a set of teeth put in for free?

Tease a lion.

121 **H**ow does a lion say hi! to other animals?

Pleased to eat you!

122 **W**hat happened to the leopard who took four baths every day?

Within a week he was spotless.

123 **W**hy did the lion feel sick after he'd eaten the priest?

Because it's hard to keep a good man down.

124 **W**hat do you call a lion wearing a fancy hat?

A dandy lion.

125 **W**hat did the lioness say to the cub chasing the hunter?

Stop playing with your food.

Dinosaurs

126 **W**hat do you get when you cross a pig with a Stegosaurus?

A porky spine.

127 **W**hy did the dinosaur fall out of a palm tree?

Because the hippopotamus pushed him out.

128 **H**ow do dinosaurs pass exams?

With extinction.

129 What dinosaur always stops to say "hi"?

An Allosaurus.

130 What's the hardest thing about making dinosaur stew?

Finding a pot big enough to put the dinosaur in.

131 What's the scariest dinosaur of all?

The Terrordactyl.

SCARY HEY?

The scariest thing in Prehistoric skies...
The Terrorsaurus

Go on, give me any word you like to spell.

Just make sure it starts with a 'B'

132 What does a Triceratops sit on?

Its Tricerabottom.

133 What's even better than a talking T-Rex?

A spelling bee.

134 **W**hy did dinosaurs eat meat?

Barbecues hadn't been invented.

135 **W**hich dinosaur could jump higher than a house?

All of them. Houses can't jump.

136 **W**hat's the best way to raise a baby dinosaur?

With a crane.

137 **H**ow do you know if there's a dinosaur in your refrigerator?

The door won't close.

138 **W**hy do museums have so many old dinosaur bones?

Because they can't find any new ones.

139 **W**hat's a dinosaur's favorite game to play with humans?

Squash.

140 **W**hat do you call a dinosaur that always uses fancy words?

A Thesaurus.

141 **W**hich dinosaur do you not invite to a sleepover?

Brontosnorus.

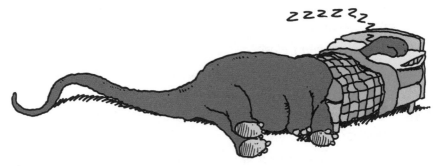

142 **W**hat's it called when a dinosaur passes gas?

A blast from the past.

143 **W**hat do dinosaurs put on their hot dogs?

Tomatosaurus.

144 **W**hat do you call a T-Rex in cowboy boots?

Tyrannosaurus Tex.

145 **W**hat do you call a T-Rex in a sombrero?

Tyrannosaurus Mex.

146 **W**hat is it called when a T-Rex has a car accident?

A Tyrannosaurus Wreck.

147 **W**hat do you get when you cross a dinosaur with explosives?

Dino-mite.

Get a load of that! There goes the last Dino-mite-o-saurus. At least he can say he went out with a BANG!

KA-BOOM

148 **W**hat do you get if you cross a Triceratops with a kangaroo?

Tricerahops.

149 **W**hat did the Apatosaurus have a long neck?

Because its feet stank.

Doctor, Doctor

150 Doctor, Doctor, I've spent so long at my computer that I now see double.

Well, walk around with one eye shut.

151 Doctor, Doctor, can I have a bottle of aspirin and a pot of glue?

Why?

Because I've got a splitting headache!

152 **D**octor, Doctor, my little brother thinks he's a computer.

Well bring him in so I can cure him.

I can't. I need to use him to finish my homework!

153 **D**octor, Doctor, I think I've been bitten by a vampire.

Drink this glass of water.

Will it make me better?

No, but I'll be able to see if your neck leaks!

154 **D**octor, Doctor, my son has swallowed my pen. What should I do?

Use a pencil until I get there.

Do you find your ears ring at all?

155 **D**octor, Doctor, I think I'm a bell.

Take these, and if they don't help, give me a ring!

156 Doctor, Doctor, I've got gas! Can you give me something?

Yes! Here's my car.

157 Doctor, Doctor, I keep thinking I'm a dog.

Sit on the couch and we'll talk about it.

But I'm not allowed on the furniture!

158 Doctor, Doctor, I think I'm a bridge.

What's come over you?

Oh, two cars, a large truck, and a bus.

159 Doctor, Doctor, I insist on getting a second opinion!

Fine, come back tomorrow.

160 Doctor, Doctor, when I press with my finger here... it hurts, and here... it hurts, and here... and here! What do you think is wrong with me?

Your finger's broken!

161 Doctor, Doctor, you have to help me out!

That's easy. Which way did you come in?

162 **D**octor, Doctor, I've swallowed my harmonica!

Well, it's a good thing you don't play the piano.

163 **D**octor, Doctor, I keep getting a pain in the eye when I drink coffee.

Have you tried taking the spoon out of the cup before you drink?

164 **D**octor, Doctor, I feel like a spoon!

Well, sit down and don't stir!

165 **D**octor, Doctor, I think I need glasses.

You certainly do. You've just walked into a restaurant!

166 **D**octor, Doctor, I feel like a dog.

Sit!

167 **D**octor, Doctor, I feel like an apple.

We must get to the core of this!

168 **D**octor, Doctor, I feel like a sheep.

That's baaaaaaaaaad!

169 **D**octor, Doctor, I'm becoming invisible.

Yes, I can see you're not all there!

170 **D**octor, Doctor, will this ointment clear up my spots?

I never make rash promises!

171 **D**octor, Doctor, everyone keeps throwing me in the garbage.

Don't talk rubbish!

172 **D**octor, Doctor, I'm boiling up!
Just simmer down!

173 **D**octor, Doctor, I feel like a needle.
I see your point!

174 **D**octor, Doctor, how can I cure my sleepwalking?
Sprinkle thumb tacks on your bedroom floor!

A GUARANTEED CURE FOR SLEEPWALKING

175 **D**octor, Doctor, I feel like a racehorse.
Take one of these every four laps!

176 **D**octor, Doctor, I feel like a bee.
Buzz off. I'm busy!

177 **D**octor, Doctor, I'm a burglar!
Have you taken anything for it?

178 **D**octor, Doctor, how can I stop my nose from running?

Stick your foot out and trip it up!

179 **D**octor, Doctor, everyone thinks I'm a liar.

Well, that's hard to believe!

180 **D**octor, Doctor, I keep thinking I'm a mosquito.

Go away, sucker!

181 **D**octor, Doctor, I keep thinking I'm a spider.

What a web of lies!

182 **D**octor, Doctor, what did the x-ray of my head show?

Absolutely nothing!

183 **D**octor, Doctor, I think I'm a snail.

Don't worry. We'll soon have you out of your shell.

184 **D**octor, Doctor, I keep painting myself gold.

Don't worry. It's just a gilt complex.

185 Doctor, Doctor, I think I'm a rubber band.

Why don't you stretch yourself out on the couch there, and tell me all about it?

186 Doctor, Doctor, I feel like a pair of curtains.

Oh, pull yourself together!

187 Doctor, Doctor, everyone keeps ignoring me.

Next please!

188 Doctor, Doctor, I think I'm a computer.

How long have you felt like this?

Ever since I was switched on!

189 Doctor, Doctor, I keep thinking there's two of me.

One at a time please!

190 Doctor, Doctor, I keep thinking I'm a computer.

My goodness, you'd better come to my office right away!

I can't. My power cable won't reach that far!

191 Doctor, Doctor, some days I feel like a tipi and other days I feel like a wigwam.

Relax, you're too tents!

192 Doctor, Doctor, my little boy has just swallowed a roll of film.

Hmmm. Let's hope nothing develops!

193 Doctor, Doctor, I can't get to sleep.

Sit on the edge of the bed, and you'll soon drop off.

194 Doctor, Doctor, I feel like a pack of cards.

I'll deal with you later!

195 Doctor, Doctor, I snore so loudly that I keep myself awake.

Sleep in another room, then.

196 **D**octor, Doctor, I have a split personality.

Well, you'd better both sit down, then.

197 **D**octor, Doctor, my sister keeps saying she feels invisible.

Which sister?

198 **D**octor, Doctor, I think I'm a yo-yo.

You're stringing me along!

199 **D**octor, Doctor, I keep thinking I'm a vampire.

Necks, please!

200 **D**octor, Doctor, I swallowed a bone.

Are you choking?

No, I really did!

201 Doctor, Doctor, I dream there are zombies under my bed. What can I do?

Saw the legs off your bed.

202 Doctor, Doctor, I think I'm a drill.

How boring for you!

203 Doctor, Doctor, I think I'm an electric eel.

That's shocking!

204 Doctor, Doctor, I think I'm a nit.

Will you get out of my hair?

205 Doctor, Doctor, I've broken my arm in two places.

Well, don't go back there again.

206 Doctor, Doctor, I think I'm a butterfly.

Will you say what you mean and stop flitting about!

207 Doctor, Doctor, I think I'm a frog.

What's wrong with that?

I think I'm going to croak!

208 **D**octor, Doctor, my hair keeps falling out. Can you give me something to keep it in?

Sure, here's a paper bag.

209 **D**octor, Doctor, I think I'm a caterpillar.

Don't worry. You'll soon change.

210 **D**octor, Doctor, these pills you gave me for B.O...

What's wrong with them?

They keep slipping out from under my arms!

211 **D**octor, Doctor, my husband smells like a fish.

Poor sole!

Jokes About Boys

212 Mom: *"Why are you scratching, Jamie?"*

Jamie: *"Because no one else knows where I itch."*

213 Did you hear about the boy who saw a witch riding on a broomstick?

He asked, *"What are you doing on that?"*

She replied, *"My sister has the vacuum cleaner!"*

Man!...Forget the broomstick and the vacuum cleaner! They ain't got nothin' on this little baby!!!

214 **D**id you hear about the dizzy Boy Scout?

He spent all day doing good turns.

215 **W**hat do you get if you cross a zombie with a Boy Scout?

A creature that scares old ladies across the street.

216 **D**id you hear about the boy who got worried when his nose grew to be 11 inches long?

He thought it might turn into a foot.

217 **D**id you hear about the little boy who was named after his father?

They called him Dad.

218 **D**id you hear about the two boys who found themselves in a modern art gallery by mistake?

"Quick," said one. *"Run, before they say we did it!"*

219 **B**oy: *"Dad, Dad, there's a monster at the door with a really ugly face!"*

Dad: "Tell him you've already got one."

220 **R**avi: *"They say ignorance is bliss."*

Rita: *"Then you should be the happiest boy in the world!"*

221 **W**hat do you get for sitting under a cow?

A pat on the head.

222 **W**hy did the boy take a pencil to bed?

To draw the curtains!

223 **W**hy was the boy unhappy to win the prize for best costume at the Halloween party?

Because he just came to pick up his little sister!

224 **W**hy did the lazy boy get a job in a bakery?

Because he wanted to loaf around!

225 **W**hich nursery rhyme boy runs upstairs and downstairs looking for cake?

Wee Little Twinkie.

226 **D**id you hear about the boy who had to do a project about trains?

He had to keep track of everything.

227 **M**other: *"Who was that on the phone, Sammy?"*

Sammy: *"No one we knew, Mom. Just some man who said it was long distance from Australia, so I told him I knew that already!"*

228 **C**harlie had a puppy on a leash. He met his brother Jim and said,

"I just got this puppy for our little brother."

"Really?" said Jim. *"That was a good trade!"*

229 **F**irst boy: *"My brother said he'd tell me everything he knows."*

Second boy: *"He must have been speechless!"*

230 **F**irst boy: *"Why is your brother always flying off the handle?"*

Second Boy: *"Because he has a screw loose!"*

231 **P**eter: *"My brother wants to work badly!"*

Anita: *"As I remember, he usually does!"*

232 **D**an: *"My little brother is a real pain."*

Nan: *"Things could be worse."*

Dan: *"How?"*

Nan: *"He could be twins!"*

233 **F**irst boy: *"Does your brother keep himself clean?"*

Second boy: *"Oh, yes. He takes a bath every month, whether he needs one or not!"*

Maybe I should bathe a little more regularly than I do...

234 **M**om: *"What are you doing, Son?"*

Boy: *"Writing my brother a letter."*

Mom: *"That's a nice idea, but why are you writing so slowly?"*

Boy: *"Because he can't read very fast!"*

235 Little brother: *"I'm going to buy a seahorse."*
Big brother: *"Why?"*
Little brother: *"Because I want to play water polo!"*

236 Big brother: *"That planet over there is Mars."*
Little brother: *"Then that other one must be Pa's."*

237 Dad: *"Don't be selfish. Let your brother use the sled half the time."*

Son: *"I do, Dad. I use it going down the hill, and he gets to use it coming up the hill!"*

238 Why did the boy go to school at night?

Because he wanted to learn to read in the dark!

239 Dad: *"Why is your January progress report so bad?"*

Son: *"Well, you know how it is. Things are always marked down after Christmas!"*

240 Why was the carpenter's son so like his father?

He was a chip off the old block.

241 Will and Bill were arguing about whose father was stronger.

Will said, *"Well, you know the Pacific Ocean? My dad dug the hole for it."*

Bill wasn't impressed.

"Well, that's nothing. You know the Dead Sea? My father's the one who killed it!"

242 Mom: *"Haven't you finished filling the salt shaker yet?"*

Son: *"Not yet. It's really hard to get the salt through all those little holes!"*

243 First witch: *"I took my boy to the zoo yesterday."*

Second witch: *"Really? Did they keep him?"*

244 "**W**illiam," said his Mom sternly. "*There were two pieces of cake in that pantry last night, and now there's only one. How do you explain that?*"

"*It was dark in the pantry,*" said William. "*And I didn't see the second piece!*"

245 "**W**hy are you crying, Ted?" asked his mom.

"*Because my new sneakers hurt,*" Ted replied.

"*That's because you've put them on the wrong feet.*"

"*But they're the only feet I have!*"

246 **A**li: "*My cat likes to drink lemonade.*"

Lenny: "*He sure must be a sourpuss!*"

247 Johnny collected lots of money from trick-or-treating and he went to the store to buy some chocolate.

"You should give that money to charity," said the shopkeeper.

"No thanks," replied Johnny. *"I'll buy the chocolate. You give the money to charity!"*

248 Boy: *"Grandpa, do you know how to croak?"*

Grandpa: *"No, I don't. Why?"*

Boy: *"Because Daddy says he'll be a rich man when you do!"*

249 Why did Matt's bicycle keep falling over?

Because it was two tired.

250 "**M**om," Richard yelled, from the kitchen.

"You know that vase you were always worried I'd break?"

"Yes, Dear. What about it?" asked his mom.

"Well...your worries are over."

Mom won't be too mad....
It's only broken into 3 big bits

251 "**M**om, there's a man at the door collecting for the old folk's home," said the little boy.

"Shall I give him Grandma?"

252 **A** young boy was helping his dad around the house.

"Son, you're like lightning with that hammer," said the father.

"Really fast, eh, Dad?" said the boy.

"No, Son. You never strike in the same place twice!"

Jokes About Girls

253 First witch: *"My, hasn't your little girl grown!"*

Second witch: *"Yes, she's certainly gruesome."*

You've grown up into the ugliest most gruesome daughter a Mom could ever want!

254 Sally: *"Can I try on that dress in the window?"*

Salesgirl: *"If you like, but most people use the dressing room."*

255 **W**hat do you call a girl with a frog on her head?

Lily!

256 **H**ow does a witch doctor ask a girl to dance?

"Voodoo like to dance with me?"

257 **W**hat kind of girl does a Mummy take on a date?

Any old girl he can dig up.

I'm going out with the boy from necks door!

258 **W**ho is a vampire likely to fall in love with?

The girl necks door.

259 **D**id you hear about the girl monster who wasn't pretty and wasn't ugly?

She was pretty ugly!

260 First girl: *"Whenever I'm down in the dumps, I buy myself a new hat."*

Second girl: *"Oh, so that's where you get them!"*

261 What is a myth?

A female moth!

262 What do young female monsters do at parties?

They go around looking for edible bachelors!

263 Have you met the girl who wanted to marry a ghost?

I can't think what possessed her!

264 Did you hear about the girl who was so hung up on road safety that she always wore white at night?

Last winter she was knocked down by a snow plow.

265   **W**hy was the Egyptian girl confused?

Because her daddy was a mummy!

266   **D**id you hear about the girl who got engaged and then found out her new fiancé had a wooden leg?

She broke it off, of course.

267   **B**ill: *"My sister has lovely long hair, all the way down her back."*

Will: *"Pity it's not on her head!"*

268   **W**hen is a chair like a woman's dress?

When it's satin.

269 **W**hy did the girl hate math?

She was a calcuhater.

270 **W**hat happened when the young wizard met the young witch?

It was love at first fright.

271 **W**hy did the girl wear a wet hat all day?

Because the label said "wash and wear".

272 **F**irst girl: *"Why are you putting your horse's saddle on backward?"*

Second girl: *"How do you know which way I'm going?"*

273 Mother: *"Why did you put a toad in your brother's bed?"*
Daughter: *"Because I couldn't find a spider."*

274 Brother: *"What happened to you?"*

Sister: *"I fell off while I was riding."*

Brother: *"Horseback?"*

Sister: *"I don't know. I'll find out when I get back to the stable."*

275 What kind of sharks never eat women?

Man-eating sharks!

276 **W**hy did the girl tiptoe past the medicine cabinet?

Because she didn't want to wake the sleeping pills.

277 **W**hy did the girl give cough syrup to the pony?

Because someone told her it was a little horse.

278 **L**ucy: *"If you eat any more ice cream, you'll burst."*

Lindy: *"Okay. Pass the ice cream and duck."*

279 **E**mma:

"What a cool pair of odd socks you have on, Jill."

Jill: *"Yes, and I have another pair just like it at home."*

280 **T**wo cannibals were having lunch.

"Your girlfriend makes a great soup," said one to the other.

"Yes!" agreed the first. *"But I'm going to miss her!"*

281 **F**irst cannibal: *"My girlfriend's a tough old bird."*

Second cannibal: *"You should have left her in the oven for another half-hour."*

282 **W**hat did the wizard say to his witch girlfriend?
Hello, gore-juice!

283 **W**hat did the undertaker say to his girlfriend?
Em-balmy about you!

284 **B**rother: *"Where was Solomon's temple?"*
Sister: *"On either side of his head."*

285 **W**hat did the skeleton say to his girlfriend?
I love every bone in your body!

286 **L**ittle Susie stood in the department store near the escalator, watching the moving handrail.

"Something wrong, little girl?" asked the security guard.

"Nope," replied Susie. *"I'm just waiting for my chewing gum to come back."*

287 Teacher: *"Sue, what letter comes after the letter A?"*
Ella: *"The rest of them."*

288 Girl: *"How much is a soft drink?"*
Waitress: *"Fifty cents."*
Girl: *"How much is a refill?"*
Waitress: *"The first is free."*
Girl: *"Well, then, I'll have a refill."*

289 **"M**ary," said her teacher. *"You can't bring that lamb into class. What about the smell?"*

"Oh, that's all right," replied Mary. *"It'll soon get used to it."*

290 Visitor: *"You're very quiet, Louise."*

Louise: *"Well, my mom gave me a dollar not to say anything about that zit on your face."*

291 Biology teacher: *"What kind of birds do we keep in captivity?"*

Janet: *"Jail birds!"*

292 **"W**hat shall we play today?" Tanya asked her best friend, Emma.

"Let's play school," said Emma.

"Okay," said Tanya. *"But I'm going to be absent."*

293 Penny: *"Will you join me in a cup of hot chocolate?"*

Mindy: *"Yes, but do you think we'll both fit?"*

294 **H**elen: *"Mom, do you know what I'm going to give you for your birthday?"*

Mom: *"No, Dear. What?"*

Helen: *"A nice teapot."*

Mom: *"But I already have a nice teapot."*

Helen: *"Not anymore. I just dropped it!"*

295 **M**om: *"Abby, quiet down. Your father can't read his paper."*

Abby: *"Wow, I'm only 8 and I can read it."*

296 **"M**rs Johnston, your daughter would be a fine dancer, except for two things."

"What are they?"

"Both left feet!"

297 **G**irl to friend: *"I'm sorry, I won't be able to come out tonight. I promised Dad I'd stay in and help him with my homework."*

Riddles

298 **W**hy was Adam the fastest runner in the history of the world?

He was first in the human race.

299 **W**hat is bigger when it's upside down?

The number 6.

300 **I**f a woman is born in Australia, grows up in China and dies in the US, what is she?

Dead.

301 What can you serve but never eat?

A tennis ball.

302 When Adam introduced himself to Eve, what three words did he use that read the same backward and forward?

"Madam, I'm Adam."

303 Why is a ladies' belt like a garbage truck?

It goes around and gathers the waist.

304 **W**hat is the difference between an oak tree and a tight shoe?

One makes acorns and the other makes corns ache.

305 **W**hich building in every city has the most stories?

The library.

306 **W**hat has ears but cannot hear?

A cornfield.

307 **W**hat kind of water cannot freeze?

Hot water.

308 **W**hat does every girl have that she can always count on?

Her fingers.

309 **A** cowboy rode into town on Friday. He stayed in town for three days and rode out on Friday. How was that possible?

Friday was the name of his horse.

310 **I**'m full of keys but I can't open any door. What am I?
A piano.

311 **W**hat has a hundred limbs but cannot walk?
A tree.

312 It starts out tall, but the longer it stands, the shorter it grows. What is it?

A candle.

A long dark night?

Sure was! I thought morning would never come.

313 How can a man go eight days without sleep?

He only sleeps at night.

314 Can you name three consecutive days without using the words Wednesday, Friday, and Sunday?

Yesterday, today, and tomorrow.

315 What occurs once in a minute, twice in a moment, and never in one thousand years?

The letter M.

316 If you are running in a race and you pass the person in second place, what place are you in?

Second place.

317 **T**hree men were in a boat when it capsized, but only two of them got their hair wet. Why?

The third man was bald.

318 **W**hat word contains 26 letters, but only three syllables?

Alphabet!

Knock, Knock

319 **K**nock, Knock.
Who's there?
Hijack!
Hijack who?
Hijack, where's Jill?

320 **K**nock, Knock.
Who's there?
Abbott!
Abbott who?
Abbott time you
opened this door!

321 **K**nock, Knock.
Who's there?
Tank.
Tank who?
You're welcome.

322 **K**nock, Knock.

Who's there?

Nobel.

Nobel who?

Nobel, that's why I knocked.

323 **K**nock, Knock.

Who's there?

Luke.

Luke who?

Luke through the peephole and find out for yourself!

324 **K**nock, Knock.

Who's there?

Adam!

Adam who?

Adam up and tell me the total!

325 **K**nock, Knock.
Who's there?
Abbey!
Abbey who?
Abbey stung me
on the nose!

326 **K**nock, Knock.
Who's there?
Olive!
Olive who?
Olive you!

327 **K**nock, Knock.
Who's there?
Abyssinia!
Abyssinia who?
Abyssinia when I get back!

328 **K**nock, Knock.
Who's there?
Beef!
Beef who?
Beef fair now!

329 **K**nock, Knock.
Who's there?
Ben!
Ben who?
Ben away a long time!

330 **K**nock, Knock.
Who's there?
Spell.
Spell who?
W-H-O.

331 **K**nock, Knock.
Who's there?
Wooden shoe.
Wooden shoe who?
Wooden shoe like to know?

Who's the new Dutch boy down the end between the Italian girl and the Aussie rubber thong?

332 **K**nock, Knock.
Who's there?
Alpaca.
Alpaca who?
Alpaca the bags. Youpaca the suitcase.

72

333 **K**nock, Knock.

Who's there?

My panther.

My panther who?

My panther falling down!

334 **K**nock, Knock.

Who's there?

Mikey.

Mikey who?

Mikey doesn't fit this keyhole.

335 **K**nock, Knock.

Who's there?

Turnip.

Turnip who?

Turnip the volume on your doorbell, I've been here for hours!

336 **K**nock, Knock.
Who's there?
Icy!
Icy who?
I see your underwear!

337 **K**nock, Knock.
Who's there?
Norma Lee.
Norma Lee who?
Norma Lee I don't knock on doors, but I was dying to meet you!

338 **K**nock, Knock.
Who's there?
Wanda.
Wanda who?
Wanda hang out with me?

339 **K**nock, Knock.
Who's there?
Boxer!
Boxer who?
Boxer tricks!

340   **K**nock, Knock.

Who's there?

Ho ho.

Ho ho who?

Your Santa Claus impression could do with a little work.

341   **K**nock, Knock.

Who's there?

A herd.

A herd who?

A herd you were home, so I thought I'd come over.

342   **K**nock, Knock

Who's there?

Doris.

Doris who?

Doris locked, that's why I'm knocking!

343   **K**nock, Knock.

Who's there?

Butcher!

Butcher who?

Butcher arms around me!

344 **K**nock, Knock.
Who's there?
Butcher!
Butcher who?
Butcher money where your mouth is!

345 **K**nock, Knock.
Who's there?
Butcher!
Butcher who?
Butcher left leg in, your left leg out!

BUTCHER LEFT LEG IN AND SHAKE IT ALL ABOUT

346 **K**nock, Knock.
Who's there?
C-2!
C-2 who?
C-2 it that you don't forget my name next time!

347 **K**nock, Knock.
Who's there?
Caesar!
Caesar who?
Caesar quickly, before she gets away!

348 **K**nock, Knock.
Who's there?
Althea!
Althea who?
Althea later alligator!

349 **K**nock, Knock.
Who's there?
Beets!
Beets who?
Beets me!

350 **K**nock, Knock.
Who's there?
Caesar!
Caesar who?
Caesar jolly good fellow!

351 **K**nock, Knock.

Who's there?

Carlotta!

Carlotta who?

Carlotta trouble when it breaks down!

352 **K**nock, Knock.

Who's there?

Canoe!

Canoe who?

Canoe come out and play with me?

353 **K**nock, Knock.

Who's there?

Carol!

Carol who?

Carol go if you turn the ignition key!

354 **K**nock, Knock.
Who's there?
Cows go!
Cows go who?
Cows go "moo", not "who"!

I just eat grass all day...
and go MOOOOO...that's what cows do!

355 **K**nock, Knock.
Who's there?
Quacker!
Quacker who?
Quacker 'nother bad joke and I'm leaving!

356 **K**nock, Knock.
Who's there?
U-8!
U-8 who?
U-8 my lunch!

357 **K**nock, Knock.
Who's there?
Cattle!
Cattle who?
Cattle always purr if you stroke it!

358 **K**nock, Knock.
Who's there?
Celeste!
Celeste who?
Celeste time I come around here if you keep me waiting any longer!

359 **K**nock, Knock.
Who's there?
Utah!
Utah who?
Utah the road and I'll paint the lines!

360 **K**nock, Knock.
Who's there?
Zany!
Zany who?
Zany body home?

361 **K**nock, Knock.
Who's there?
Zeke!
Zeke who?
Zeke and you shall find!

362 **K**nock, Knock.
Who's there?
X!
X who?
X-tremely pleased to meet you!

363 **K**nock, Knock.
Who's there?
Hans!
Hans who?
Hans broken since I shook yours!

364 **K**nock, Knock.
Who's there?
Xavier!
Xavier who?
Xavier money for a rainy day!

365 **K**nock, Knock.
Who's there?
Xavier!
Xavier who?
Xavier breath, I'm not leaving!

366 **K**nock, Knock.
Who's there?
Barbara!
Barbara who?
Barbara black sheep, have you any wool!

367 **K**nock, Knock.
Who's there?
Zia!
Zia who?
Zia in a minute!

368 **K**nock, Knock.
Who's there?
Jaws!
Jaws who?
Jaws truly!

369 **K**nock, Knock.
Who's there?
Jam!
Jam who?
Jam mind, I'm trying to get out!

370 **K**nock, Knock.
Who's there?
Jilly!
Jilly who?
Jilly out here, so let me in!

371 **K**nock, Knock.
Who's there?
Jim!
Jim who?
Jim mind if we come in?

372 **K**nock, Knock.
Who's there?
Jimmy!
Jimmy who?
Jimmy a little kiss on the cheek!

373 **K**nock, Knock.
Who's there?
Gary!
Gary who?
Gary on smiling!

374 **K**nock, Knock.
Who's there?
Ahmed!
Ahmed who?
Ahmed a mistake!
I meant to knock next door.

Just a happy guy

kissy
kissy
kissy

375 **K**nock, Knock.
Who's there?
Avon!
Avon who?
Avon you to
open the door!

376 **K**nock, Knock.
Who's there?
Gizza!
Gizza who?
Gizza kiss!

377 **K**nock, Knock.
Who's there?
Aida!
Aida who?
Aida whole box of cookies and now I feel sick!

378 **K**nock, Knock.
Who's there?
Artichokes!
Artichokes who?
Artichokes when he eats too fast!

379 **K**nock, Knock.
Who's there?
Alaska!
Alaska who?
Alaska one more time: please let me in!

380 **K**nock, Knock.
Who's there?
Alf!
Alf who?
Alf all if you
don't catch me!

381 **K**nock, Knock.
Who's there?
Arch!
Arch who?
Bless you!

382 **K**nock, Knock.

Who's there?

Alex!

Alex who?

Alex-plain later. Just let me in!

383 **K**nock, Knock.

Who's there?

Abbot!

Abbot who?

Abbot you don't know who's knocking!

384 **K**nock, Knock.

Who's there?

Bacon!

Bacon who?

Bacon a cake for
your birthday!

385 **K**nock, Knock.

Who's there?

Amos!

Amos who?

Amosquito!

386 **K**nock, Knock.

Who's there?

Anne!

Anne who?

Anne-other mosquito!

387 **K**nock, Knock.

Who's there?

Adore!

Adore who?

Adore is between us. Open up!

388 **K**nock, Knock.

Who's there?

Ammonia!

Ammonia who?

Ammonia little girl and I can't reach the doorbell!

389 **K**nock, Knock.

Who's there?

Avon!

Avon who?

Avon you to let me in!

390 **K**nock, Knock.

Who's there?

Armageddon!

Armageddon who?

Armageddon out of here if you won't let me in!

391 **K**nock, Knock.

Who's there?

Acute!

Acute who?

Acute little boy!

392 **K**nock, Knock.
Who's there?
Bernadette!
Bernadette who?
Bernadette my lunch and now I'm starving!

393 **K**nock, Knock.
Who's there?
Bolton!
Bolton who?
Bolton the door. That's why I can't get in!

394 **K**nock, Knock.
Who's there?
Ben Hur!
Ben Hur who?
Ben Hur over an hour. Let me in!

395 **K**nock, Knock.
Who's there?
Arncha!
Arncha who?
Arncha going to let me in? It's freezing out here!

396 **K**nock, Knock.
Who's there?
Beth!
Beth who?
Beth wisheth, thweetie!

397 **K**nock, Knock.
Who's there?
Radio.
Radio who?
Radio not, here
I come!

28...29... 30,
Here I come!
Over and out...

398 **K**nock, Knock.
Who's there?
A chicken!

399 **K**nock, Knock.
Who's there?
Another chicken!

400 **K**nock, Knock.
Who's there?
Cargo!
Cargo who?
Cargo beep-beep! No more chickens.

401 **K**nock, Knock.
Who's there?
Isabel!
Isabel who?
Isabel broken 'cos I had to knock!

402 **K**nock, Knock.
Who's there?
Adair!
Adair who?
Adair once, but I'm bald now!

403 **K**nock, Knock.
Who's there?
Chicken!
Chicken who?
Chicken your pocket. My keys might be there!

404 **K**nock, Knock.
Who's there?
Cantaloupe!
Cantaloupe who?
Cantaloupe with you tonight!

405 **K**nock, Knock.
Who's there?
Cook!
Cook who?
Don't you make a mighty fine clock?

406 **K**nock, Knock.
Who's there?
Cash!
Cash who?
You're nuts!

407 **K**nock, Knock.
Who's there?
Dwayne!
Dwayne who?
Dwayne the
bathtub before
I dwown!

408 **K**nock, Knock.
Who's there?
Debate!
Debate who?
Debate goes on de hook if you want to catch de fish!

409 **K**nock, Knock.
Who's there?
Des!
Des who?
Des no bell so I had to knock!

410 **K**nock, Knock.
Who's there?
Don!
Don who?
Don just stand there, open the door!

411 **K**nock, Knock.
Who's there?
Doctor!
Doctor who?
That's right!

412 **K**nock, Knock.
Who's there?
Despair!
Despair who?
Despair tire is flat.
Can you help me
out?

413 **K**nock, Knock.
Who's there?
Danielle!
Danielle who?
Danielle so loud, I can hear you just fine!

414 **K**nock, Knock.
Who's there?
Euripides!
Euripides who?
Euripides pants, Eumenides pants!

415 **K**nock, Knock.
Who's there?
Europe!
Europe who?
Europen this door so I can come in!

416 **K**nock, Knock.
Who's there?
Letter!
Letter who?
Letter in or she'll knock the door down!

...and whatever you do.... don't call her 'dear'...

417 **K**nock, Knock.
Who's there?
Ferdie!
Ferdie who?
Ferdie last time open this door!

418 **K**nock, Knock.
Who's there?
Fanny!
Fanny who?
Fanny how you keep asking, "Who's there?"

419 **K**nock, Knock.
Who's there?
Figs!
Figs who?
Figs the doorbell. It's been broken for ages!

420 **K**nock, Knock.
Who's there?
Fozzie!
Fozzie who?
Fozzie hundredth time, it's me!

421 **K**nock, Knock.
Who's there?
Felix!
Felix who?
Felix my ice cream, I'll lick his!

422 **K**nock, Knock.
Who's there?
Gino!
Gino who?
Gino how long I've been waiting out here?

423 **K**nock, Knock.
Who's there?
Gopher!
Gopher who?
Gopher help. I've been tied up!

424 **K**nock, Knock.
Who's there?
Gus!
Gus who?
No, you guess who. I already know who I am!

425 **K**nock, Knock.
Who's there?
Gorilla!
Gorilla who?
Gorilla cheese
sandwich for
me, gorgeous!

426 **K**nock, Knock.
Who's there?
Howard!
Howard who?
Howard I know!

427 **K**nock, Knock.
Who's there?
Ivan!
Ivan who?
Ivan-other thousand knock-knock jokes. Would you
like to hear them?

Science

428 How does a scientist freshen her breath?

Experi-mints.

429 Why did the cloud date the fog?

Because he was so down-to-earth.

430 What did the chemistry teacher say to the student?

I'm in my element.

431 How do you organize a space party?

You planet.

432 **W**hat did the lonely germ say?

Is there antibody out there?

433 **W**hy did the dinosaur cross the road?

The chicken hadn't evolved yet.

434 **W**hat did one DNA strand say to the other DNA strand?

Do these genes make my butt look big?

435 **W**hat did the scientist do when nobody laughed at his jokes?

He kept trying until he got a reaction.

436 **W**hat do you get if you buy one proton and one electron?

One neutron free of charge!

437 **H**ow did Benjamin Franklin feel when he discovered electricity?

Shocked!

438 **W**hat did the mountain say to the volcano?

You're hot!

439 **W**hat did the volcano say back?

You rock!

440 **W**hy did the scientist break up with her boyfriend?

There was no chemistry.

441 **W**hat did the proton break up with the electron?
He was sick of her negativity.

442 **W**hat do you get if you break the laws of gravity?
A suspended sentence.

443 **W**hite kind of dog does a scientist have?
A lab.

444 **W**hy is chemistry different to cooking?
In chemistry you never *lick the spoon.*

445 **W**hy did the magnets break up?
Because they were polar opposites.

446 **W**hy are chemists great problem solvers?
They have all the solutions!

447 **W**hich elements love to rock out?
Heavy metals.

448 **W**hy did the bacteria cross the microscope?
To get to the other slide.

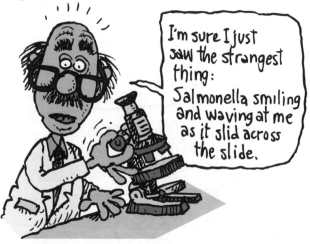

I'm sure I just saw the strangest thing: Salmonella smiling and waving at me as it slid across the slide.

449 **W**hat did the pot say to the boiling water?
You will be mist.

450 **H**ow often does the science teacher make bad jokes?
Only periodically.

451 **H**ow does the moon cut his hair?
Eclipse it.

452 **W**hat did one plant do when the other plant was sad?

Photosympathize.

453 **W**hat did one wind turbine say to the other wind turbine?

I'm a big fan.

454 **W**hat is a physicist's favorite food?

Fission chips.

455 **H**ow did the professor lose an electron?

He didn't keep an ion it.

456 **D**id you hear about the party on the moon?

There was no atmosphere.

457 **W**hat did the rock say to his girlfriend?

Don't take me for granite!

458 **W**hat's the difference between a dog and a marine biologist?

One wags a tail and the other tags a whale.

459 **W**hat did the thigh bone say to the shin bone?

I kneed you.

460 **I**f water is H2O, what is H2O4?

Drinking.

461 **W**hy did the grain of wheat want to know the secret of life?

He was a complex carbohydrate.

462 **W**hat did the student say when her teacher threw sodium chloride at her?

That's a salt.

463 **W**hat did the abacus say to the math teacher?

You can count on me!

464 **W**hy should you never trust an atom?

Because they make up everything.

Miscellaneous

465   **W**hich king invented fractions?
Henry the 1/8.

466   **W**hy did the picture go to jail?
It was framed!

467   **W**hat did the
policeman say to
his belly button?
*You're under a
vest.*

468   **W**hat did the big
flower say to the
little flower?
Hi, bud!

469   **W**hat sits in the
middle of the
world wide web?
*A very, very big
spider.*

470 **D**id you hear about the monkey who left bits of his lunch all over the house?

His dad went bananas.

471 **H**ow do you stop your laptop batteries from running out?

Hide their sneakers!

472 **W**hat music frightens balloons?

Pop music.

473 **"I** bought this computer yesterday and I found a twig in the thumb drive!"

"I'm sorry, Sir. You'll have to speak to the branch manager."

474 How do you make a potato puff?

Chase it around the garden.

475 What kind of shoes do ninjas wear?

Sneakers!

476 What do the invention of the parachute and its first trial-run have in common?

They were both groundbreaking.

I should have taken that second set of lounge room curtains to use. I fear one is not enough!

477 How do you talk to a giant?

Use really big words.

478 Why did the kid cross the playground?

To get to the other slide.

479 What does a cloud wear under his raincoat?

Thunderwear.

480 How does Darth Vader like his toast?

On the dark side.

481 **W**hat vegetable goes well with jacket potatoes?

Button mushrooms.

482 **W**hy didn't the waffle go to the pancake party?

It was too square.

483 **W**hy are stairs so untrustworthy?

They're always up to something.

484 **W**hat did the mouse say to the keyboard?

You're just my type!

485 **W**hat do you call cheese that isn't yours?

Nacho cheese!

486 **W**hat do you call an old snowman?

A puddle.

487 **W**hat did Charles Dickens keep in his spice rack?
The best of thymes, the worst of thymes.

488 **W**hy did the yogurt go to the art gallery?
It was cultured.

489 **W**hat do ghosts like to eat in the summer?
I scream.

490 **W**hat did the flower say after it told a joke?
I was just pollen yer leg.

491 **W**hat do cows listen to?
Moosic.

492 **W**hy are giraffes good friends to have?
Because they stick their neck out for you.

493 **W**hat do you call a boomerang that doesn't come back?

A stick.

494 **W**hich knight invented the round table?

Sir Cumference.

495 **W**hat musical instrument is found in the bathroom?

A tuba toothpaste.

496 **W**hat do you call two banana skins?

Slippers.

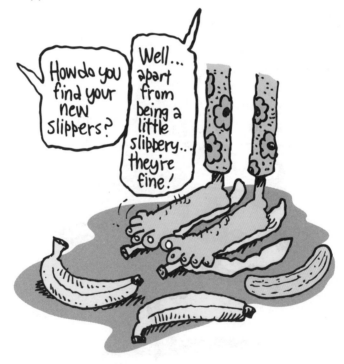

497 **W**hat kind of award did the dentist receive?

A plaque.

498 **W**hat's the difference between roast meat and pea soup?

Anyone can roast meat.

499 **W**hat did the mommy volcano say to the baby volcano.

I lava you.

500 **H**ow do spiders get married?

They have webbings.

501 **W**hat do you get when you cross an orange with a squash court?

Orange squash.

502 **W**hat time is it when someone throws bread at your head?

Time to duck.

503 **W**hat time is it when a ball goes through a window?

Time to get a new window.

504 **W**hat did the mathematician say to the man who invented zero?

"Thanks for nothing!"

505 **W**hat did Baby Corn say to Mama Corn?

Where is Pop Corn?

506 **W**hat did one banana say to the other banana?

Nothing. Bananas can't talk.

507 **W**hy was the glow worm unhappy?

Her children weren't very bright.

508 **W**hat's the hottest letter in the alphabet?

It's "b", because it makes oil boil!

509 **W**hat's a pirate's favorite letter?

Arrrrrrrrrr.

510 **W**hat's the difference between Santa Claus and a warm dog?

Santa wears the suit, but a warm dog just pants.

511 **W**hy did the farmer plow his field with a steamroller?

He wanted to grow mashed potatoes.

512 **W**hy did the cookie go to the hospital?

Because he felt crummy.

513 **W**hat's small and green and goes camping?

A boy sprout.

514 **W**hat did one plate say to the other plate?

"Dinner is on me!"

515 **H**ow do you stop an astronaut's baby from crying?

You rocket!

516 **W**hat's the difference between a night watchman and a butcher?

One stays awake and the other weighs a steak!

517 **W**here do you learn to make ice cream?

Sundae school.

518 **W**here do hamburgers go dancing?

A meatball.

519 **W**hy can't your hand be 12 inches long?

Because then it would be a foot.

520 What's a king's favorite weather?

Reign.

521 How do cows get so many bargains?

They read cattle-logs.

522 Why is a bad joke like a blunt pencil?

It has no point.

523 What do you call a fly without wings?

A walk.

524 How did the hairdresser win the race?

She knew a shortcut.

525 **W**hat did the hat say to the cap?

Wait here, I'm going on ahead.

526 **W**hat kind of bug is in the CIA?

A spy-der.

527 **W**hy is a bad joke like a rotten cabbage?

It's a stinker!

528 Why was the cupcake so quiet?

It had muffin much to say.

529 What do you get when you put cheese next to a duck?

Cheese and quackers.

530 What's green, covered in ice cream, and sad?

Apple grumble.

531 What did one wall say to the other wall?

I'll meet you at the corner.

532 Why couldn't the pirate learn the alphabet?

He was always lost at C.

533 **W**hy is dark spelled with a K and not a C?
Because you can't C in the dark.

534 **W**hy was the broom late to school?
It over-swept.

535 **W**hat has hands but can't clap?
A clock.

536 **W**hat did one toilet say to another toilet?
You look a bit flushed.

537 What happened when there was a fight in the seafood restaurant?

Two fish got battered.

Yes officer, the two pieces of fish were battered, and I was nearly salted but managed to get away.

538 What's the difference between a young lady and a fresh loaf?

One is a well-bred maid and the other is well-made bread.

539 Duck: "Do you have any lip gloss?"

Storekeeper: *"Yes, of course. Will that be cash or credit?"*

Duck: *"Just put it on my bill."*

Where all the slow tomatoes end up.

540 What did one tomato say to the one behind him?

Ketchup!

541 What's one good thing about Switzerland?

Well, the flag is a big plus.

542 What time does Godzilla go to school?
Time to run!

543 **W**hy was the egg thrown out of class?

He told too many yolks.

544 **W**hy did the cantaloupe jump in the lake?

It wanted to be a watermelon.

545 **W**hat did the mother hamburger name her baby hamburger?

Patty.

546 **W**hat do you call a man with a shovel in his head?

Doug.

547 **W**hat do you call a man without a shovel in his head?

Douglas.

548 **W**hat falls but never hits the ground?

The temperature.

549 **W**hy did the jalapeno knit herself a cardigan?

Because she was a little chili.

550 **W**hat do baseball and pancakes have in common?

They both need a good batter.

551 **I**f a seagull flies over the sea, what flies over the bay?

A bagel.

552 **W**hat time do ducks wake up?

The quack of dawn.

553 What was the lazy boy's favorite type of exercises?

Didley-squats.

554 Why did the man dress up as a pancake for Halloween?

He wanted to give everyone the crêpes.

555 What do you call a line of rabbits hopping backwards?

A receding hare line.

556 What did the 0 say to the 8?

"Nice belt!"

557 When does "B" come after "U"?

When you steal its honey.

558 What are the names of the small rivers that run into the Nile?

The juve-niles.

559 **H**ow do elves eat pancakes?

In short stacks.

560 **W**hat do you know about the Dead Sea?

Dead? I didn't even know it was sick!

561 **W**hy is the Mississippi such an unusual river?

It has four eyes and can't even see.

562 **W**here is the English Channel?

Not sure. It's not on my T.V.

563 **W**hy does the Statue of Liberty stand in New York Harbor?

Because it can't sit down.

564 **W**hat fur do we get from a tiger?

As fur as possible.

565 What are the creepiest letters in the alphabet?

I.C.U.

566 What birds are found in Portugal?

Portu-geese.

567 What did the farmer say when he lost his tractor?

Where's my tractor?

568 Name three famous poles.

North, south, and tad.

569 What do you do with crude oil?

Teach it some manners.

570 Why did the shark spit out the clown fish?

It tasted funny.

571 What did the traffic light say to the car?

"Don't look, I'm about to change!"

572 **W**hat do you call a magical dog?

A Labracadabrador.

573 **W**hat do you call someone who welcomes you home every day?

Matt.

574 **W**hat did the pirate say on his eightieth birthday?

Aye matey!

575 **W**hy did the frog take the bus.

Because the car got toad.

576 **W**hy did the girl write an apology letter in dots and dashes?

It was in re-morse code.

577 **H**ow do aliens hold their pants up?

Asteroid belts.

578 **W**hy don't aliens play golf in space?

Too many black holes.

579 **W**hat do you get from a pampered cow?

Spoiled milk.

580 **W**hy did the pig have ink on its face?

It had been in the pen.

581 **W**hat smells funny?

Clown poo.

582 **W**hy didn't the shrimp share?

Because he was a little shellfish.

583 **W**hat do you do with a sick boat?

Take it to the dock.

584 **W**hy did the fence builder get fired?

Because he deserted his posts.

585 **W**hat do you call an amorous insect?

A love bug!

586 **W**hy can't you hear a Pterodactyl going to the bathroom?

Because the "P" is silent.

587 **W**hat do stars do in the bathroom?

Twinkle.

Do You Want to Hear a Joke About...

588 . . . an electric drill?
It's too boring.

589 ... a pizza?
It's too cheesy.

590 ... the garbage collector?
It's really rubbish.

Those jokes of yours are terrible Ivan!

They're meant to be terrible!

591 ... Tsar Ivan?
It's really terrible.

592 ... the one-note tune?

It's very monotonous.

593 ... a rainy day?

It's too dreary.

594 ... the electric wire?

It's too shocking!

595 ... a cemetery?

It's very grave.

596 ... the haunted house?

It's quite frightful.

597 ... the spoiled fruit?

It's pretty rotten.

598 ... a chicken?

It's too fowl.

599 ... a watermelon?

It's a bit seedy.

600 ... the fish-flavored ice cream?

It's in very poor taste.

601 ... a security system?

It's alarming.

602 ... an unpolished diamond?

It's very dull.

Monsters, Witches, Ghosts, and Vampires

603 **W**hat do you call a monster airline steward?
A fright attendant.

604 **W**hy did the monster buy an ax?
Because he wanted to get ahead in life.

605 **W**hat is a monster's favorite game?
Hide and Shriek.

606 **W**hat do Italian monsters eat?
Spookgetti.

607 What do Hungarian monsters eat?

Ghoulash.

608 What do you do with a blue monster?

Try to cheer him up a bit.

609 Why did the monster comedian like playing to skeletons?

Because he knew how to tickle their funny bones.

610 What do you call a monster that comes to collect your laundry?

An undie-taker.

611 If you crossed the Loch Ness monster with a shark, what would you get?

Loch Jaws.

612 What eats its victims two by two?

Noah's Shark.

613 **W**hich monster is the most untidy?

The Loch Mess Monster.

614 **D**uring which age did Mummies live?

The Band-Age.

615 **W**hy was the monster catching centipedes?

He wanted scrambled legs for breakfast.

616 **W**hat does a ghost call his Mom and Dad?
His transparents.

617 **W**hat should you take if a monster invites you to dinner?

Someone who can't run as fast as you.

618 **H**ow does Frankenstein eat?

He bolts his food down.

619 **W**hat's a good job for a stylish monster?

A scare-dresser.

620 What do you think when you see a monster?

"I hope he hasn't seen me!"

621 What did the metal monster want on his gravestone?

Rust in Peace.

622 Where do skeletons keep their money?

In a joint account.

623 Why didn't the skeleton go bungee jumping?

He didn't have the guts.

624 What do you do if a monster rolls his eyes at you?

Just pick them up and roll them back!

625 **W**hy did the young monster take a runner to school in his lunch?

Because he liked fast food.

626 **W**hat monster roams in the forest?

Frankenpine.

627 **W**ho patrols cemeteries at night?

A fright watchman.

628 **W**hat do you have to buy if you invite monsters around for a party?

A new house.

629 What is a monster's favorite craft?

Tie and die.

630 What do ghosts use to type letters?

A type-frighter.

631 What type of horses do monsters ride?

Night mares.

632 Why can't ghosts tell lies?

You can see right through them.

633 What do monsters like reading in the papers every day?

Their horror-scopes, of course!

634 **W**hat's a monster's favorite shape?
A vicious circle.

635 **W**hat type of music do Mummies prefer?
Wrap music.

636 **W**hy did the friendly monster get a fine?
For driving scarelessly.

637 **W**hat feature do witches love on their computers?
The spell-checker.

638 **W**hat does a Yeti eat for dinner?
An ice burger.

639 Does a monster need a menu while vacationing on a cruise ship?

No, just the passenger list.

640 How do you talk to the Loch Ness monster when he's so far under water?

Drop him a line.

COME ON UP SO WE CAN TAKE YOUR PHOTO!

641 What did the monster say when he saw a rush-hour train full of passengers?

Great! A chew-chew train!

642 Why did the monster eat the lamp?

He wanted some light refreshment.

BRUTE AFTER SHAVE

643 What aftershave do monsters prefer?

Brute.

644 How do you know there's a monster in your shower?

You can't close the shower curtain.

645 **W**hat should you do if a monster runs through your front door?

Run out the back door.

646 **W**hy did the young monster knit herself three socks?

She grew another foot.

647 **F**irst monster: *"I've just changed my mind."*

Second monster: *"Does it work better than the old one?"*

648 **O**n which day do monsters eat people?

Chewsday.

649 **W**hat does a monster Mommy say to her kids at dinner time?

Don't speak with someone in your mouth.

650 **H**ow do you stop a charging monster?

Take away his credit card.

651 **W**hat's the name of a clever monster?

Frank Einstein.

652 **H**ow did the monster cure his sore throat?

By gargoyling every day.

653 **T**he police are looking for a monster with one eye.

They should use two!

654 **D**id you hear what happened to Ray when he met the man-eating monster?

He became an ex-Ray!

655 **W**hy was the big, hairy, two-headed monster top of the school class?

Because two heads are better than one.

656 **W**hy did the monster fail music class?

His Bach was worse than his bite.

657 **S**mall monster: *"Dad, the dentist wasn't painless like he said he'd be."*

Dad monster: *"Did he hurt you?"*

Small monster: *"No, but he yelled when I bit his finger!"*

658 **W**hat did Dracula call his son?

Fang.

659 **W**hich of the witches' friends eats the fastest?

The goblin.

660 **W**hat do you call a kind and pretty witch?

A failure.

661 **W**hy do demons and ghouls get on so well?

Because demons are a ghoul's best friend.

662 **H**ow does a skeleton call his friends?

On a telebone.

663 **W**as Dracula ever married?

No, he was a bat-chelor!

664 **W**hat do you get if you cross a vampire with Al Capone?

A fangster!

665 **W**hy are skeletons usually so calm?

Nothing gets under their skin!

666 **W**hy do skeletons hate winter?

Because the cold goes right to their bones!

667 **W**hat does Dracula get in the mailbox?

Fang mail!

668 **W**hat do you call an old and foolish vampire?

A silly old sucker!

a silly old sucker

669 **W**hy do dragons sleep during the day?

So they can fight knights!

670 **W**hat should you say when you meet a ghost?

How do you boo, Sir?

671 **W**hat would you find on a haunted beach?

A sand witch!

AAAARRR!

Don't do that! It scares the living daylights out of me

672 **W**hen do ghosts usually appear?

Just before someone screams!

673 **W**hat do you think of Dracula films?

Fangtastic!

674 **W**hy are graveyards so noisy?

Because of all the coffin!

Silly Inventions

680 Silent alarm clock

681 Fireproof matches

682 Inflatable dartboard

683 Pedal-powered wheelchair

684 Double-sided playing cards

685 Submarine screen door

686 Light-activated torch

687 Powdered water

688 **W**aterproof teabag

689 **H**and-powered chainsaw

690 **E**jector seat in a helicopter

691 **S**eatbelt for motorbikes

692 **I**ndex in a dictionary

School Jokes

693 **D**id you hear about the student who said he couldn't write an essay on goldfish because he didn't have any waterproof ink?

...Or, the sewing teacher who had her students in stitches?

...Or, maybe, the cooking teacher who thought Hamlet was an omelet with bacon?

694 **W**hat would you get if you crossed a teacher with a vampire?

Lots of blood tests.

NOW... Your BLOOD TEST has come back TYPE A ... Top marks!

695 **T**eacher: *"I hope I didn't see you copying from John's exam paper, James."*

James: *"I hope you didn't see me either!"*

696 Laugh, and the class laughs with you.

But you get detention alone.

697 Teacher: "What came after the Stone Age and the Bronze Age?"

Student: "The saus-age."

698 Teacher: *"What family does the octopus belong to?"* Student: *"Nobody's I know."*

699 **H**ow do you get a math teacher to bake you a cake?
Tell them it's as easy as pi.

700 **D**id you hear about the cross-eyed teacher?
He couldn't control his pupils.

701 **T**eacher: *"What's the name of a liquid that won't freeze?"*
Student: *"Hot water."*

702 **T**eacher: *"If I bought 100 buns for a dollar, what would each bun be?"*
Student: *"Old and stale."*

703 **T**eacher: *"Can anyone tell me what the Dog Star is?"*
Student: *"Lassie."*

704 How do you make seven an even number?

Take off the s.

705 What is the easiest way to get a day off school?

Wait until Saturday.

706 How many letters are in the alphabet?

Eleven. Count them t-h-e-a-l-p-h-a-b-e-t!

707 What is the robot's favorite part of school?

Assembly.

708 Why can you believe everything a bearded teacher tells you?

They can't tell bald-faced lies.

709 Did you hear about the teacher who wore sunglasses to give out exam results?

He took a dim view of his students' performance.

710 How does a math teacher know how long she sleeps?

She takes a ruler to bed.

711 What do you call an art teacher who is always complaining?

Mona Lisa.

712 Math teacher: *"Anne, why have you brought a picture of the queen of England with you today?"*

Anne: *"You told us to bring a ruler with us."*

713 What type of instruments did the early Britons play?

The Anglo-saxophone.

714 Math teacher: *"Richard, if you had 50 cents in each pants pocket, and $2 in each jacket pocket, what would you have?"*

Richard: *"Someone else's clothes, Sir."*

715 Teacher: *"You missed school yesterday, didn't you?"*

Student: *"Not very much."*

716 Student: *"I didn't do my homework because I lost my memory."*

Teacher: *"When did this start?"*

Student: *"When did what start?"*

717 Teacher: *"I told you to stand at the end of the line."*

Student: *"I tried, but someone was already there."*

718 Teacher: *"I told you to draw a cow eating grass, but you've only drawn a cow."*

Student: *"The cow has eaten all the grass."*

719 Did you hear about the two history teachers who were dating?

They go to restaurants to talk about old times.

720 Teacher: *"Why haven't you been to school for the past two weeks, Billy?"*

Billy: *"It's not my fault. Whenever I go to cross the road outside, there's a man with a sign saying 'Stop Children Crossing'!"*

721 Math teacher: *"If you multiplied 1,386 by 395, what would you get?"*

Student: *"The wrong answer."*

722 **W**hy did the boy throw his watch out of the window during a test?

Because he wanted to make time fly.

723 **E**nglish teacher: *"James, give me a sentence with the word 'counterfeit' in it."*

James: *"I wasn't sure if she was a centipede or a millipede, so I had to count her feet."*

724 **C**omputer teacher: *"Sarah, give me an example of software."*

Sarah: *"A floppy hat."*

725 **"W**hat were you before you started school, girls and boys?"* asked the teacher, hoping that someone would say *"babies".*

She was disappointed when all the children cried out, *"Happy!"*

Before I came to school this morning... I was a tadpole.

726 **B**en's teacher thinks Ben is a wonder child.

She wonders whether he'll ever learn anything.

727 "*I'm not going to school today,*" said Alexander to his mother. "*The teachers bully me and the boys don't like me.*"

"*That's not too surprising. You're 35 years old,*" replied his mother, "*and you're the principal!*"

728 Silly Simon was writing a geography essay for his teacher. It began like this: *The people who live in Paris are called parasites . . .*

729 Teacher: "*Are you good at arithmetic?*"

Mary: "*Well, yes and no.*"

Teacher: "*What do you mean, yes and no?*"

Mary: "*Yes, I'm no good at arithmetic.*"

730 Cooking teacher: "*Joe, what are the best things to put in a chocolate cake?*"

Joe: "*Teeth!*"

731 Teacher: *"Your daughter's only 5 and she can spell her name backwards? Why, that's remarkable!"*

Mother: *"Yes, we're very proud of her."*

Teacher: *"And what is your daughter's name?"*

Mother: *"Anna."*

732 **"W**hat are three words most often used by students?" the teacher asked the class.

"I don't know," sighed a student.

"That's correct!" said the teacher.

733 Teacher: *"Stop pulling faces, Billy. I was told when I was young that if I kept making ugly faces, my face would stay that way."*

Billy: *"Well, I can see you didn't listen."*

734 Shane: *"Dad, today my teacher yelled at me for something I didn't do."*

Dad: *"What did he yell at you for?"*

Shane: *"For not doing my homework."*

735 Teacher: *"If you had one dollar and asked your dad for one dollar, how much money would you have?"*

Student: *"One dollar."*

Teacher: *"Are you sure?"*

Student: *"Yes, my dad wouldn't give me a dollar."*

Silly Book Titles

736 *My Golden Wedding* by Annie Versary

737 *The Terrible Problem* by Major Setback

738 *A Load of Old Rubbish* by Stephan Nonsense

739 *Don't Leave Without Me* by Isa Coming

740 *When Shall We Meet Again?* by Miles Apart

741 *The Atlantic Ocean* by I. C. Waters

742 *Will He Win?* by Betty Wont

743 *Hair Disorders* by Dan Druff

811 *Ghosts and Ghouls* by Sue Pernatural

812 *Swallowing Dr Jekyll's Potion* by Iris Keverything

813 *A Ghost in My House* by Olive N. Fear

814 *Adding Up* by Juan and Juan

815 *The Chocolate Bar* by Ken I. Havesome

816 *The Lady Artist* by Andrew Pictures

817 *The Leaky Tap* by Constance Dripping

818 *In the Summer* by Clement Weather

819 *Telephone Problems* by Ron Number

829 *Crossing Roads Safely* by Luke Bothways

830 *Keeping Pet Snakes* by Sir Pent

831 *The Omen* by B. Warned

832 *The Bad Tempered Werewolf* by Claudia Armoff

833 *The Vampire's Victim* by E. Drew Blood

834 *Never Make a Witch Angry* by Sheila Tack

835 *Ghost Stories* by I.M. Scared

836 *Hunting Vampires* by Count Miout

Space

860 **W**hy did the boy become an astronaut?
Because he had his head in the stars.

861 **W**hat creates the most housework in alien homes?
Stardust.

862 **W**here do astronauts leave their space ships?
At parking meteors!

863 **W**hat do you call the bugs on the moon?
Luna-tics

864 How do you get a baby astronaut to sleep?

You rock-et!

865 What's an astronaut's favorite game?

Moonopoly!

866 How do spacemen pass the time on long trips?

They play astronauts and crosses!

867 Why does meat taste better in space?

Because it's meteor!

868 First astronaut: *"I'm hungry."*

Second astronaut: *"So am I. It must be launch time."*

869 **C**an I have a return ticket to the moon please?
Sorry the moon's full tonight.

870 **W**hat do you call a space magician?
A flying sorcerer!

871 **"I** want to be an astronaut when I grow up."
"What high hopes you have!"

872 **W**hat did the alien say to the gas pump?
"Don't you know it's rude to stick your finger in your ear?"

873 **H**ow does a robot alien shave?
With a laser blade!

874 **W**hat do you call a robot who takes the long way around?

R2 Detour!

875 **W**hat holds the moon up?

Moonbeams!

Sport

876 **W**hat job does Dracula have with the Transylvanian baseball team?

He's the bat boy.

Now when you get out there... I want to see HOME RUNS from you guys!

877 **W**hy is bowling the quietest sport?

Because you can hear a pin drop.

878 "I can't see us ever finishing this bowling game."

"Why is that?"

"Every time I knock all the pins down, someone calls a strike!"

879 When is a baby like a basketball player?

When he dribbles!

880 What part of a football field smells the best?

The scenter spot!

881 Why aren't sports stadiums built in outer-space?

Because there is no atmosphere!

882 Which goalkeeper can jump higher than a crossbar?

All of them. A crossbar can't jump!

883 **W**hat are Brazilian soccer fans called?

Brazil nuts!

884 **W**here do football players dance?

At a foot ball!

885 **W**hat sort of nails do you find in football shoes?

Toenails.

886 **H**ow do you start a doll's race?

Ready, Teddy, Go!

887 Why wouldn't the coach let elephants on the swim team?

He was afraid they would drop their trunks.

888 How do hens encourage their favorite basketball teams?

They egg them on!

889 Who won the race between two balls of string?

They were tied!

890 How did the basketball court get wet?

The players dribbled all over it!

891 **W**hy don't grasshoppers go to baseball games?
They prefer a game of cricket.

892 **W**hy didn't the dog want to play football?
It was a boxer!

893 **W**hy does a polo player ride a horse?
Because they're too heavy to carry.

894 **H**ow do you stop squirrels from playing football in the yard?

Hide the ball, it drives them nuts!

895 **W**hy should you be careful when playing against a team of big cats?

They might be cheetahs!

896 **W**hy do football coaches bring suitcases along to away games?

So that they can pack the defense!

897 **W**hy was the team manager shaking the cat?

To see if there was any money in the kitty!

898 **W**here do football coaches go when they are sick of the game?

The bored room!

899 **C**oach: *"Our new player cost $10 million. I call him our wonder player."*

Fan: *"Why's that?"*

Coach: *"Every time he plays, I wonder why I bothered to draft him!"*

900 **C**oach: *"I'll give you $100 a week to start, and $500 a week in a year."*

Baseball player: *"See you in a year!"*

901 **W**hy do artists never win when they play basketball?

They keep drawing the foul!

902 **W**hat did they call Dracula when he refereed the World Series?

The Vumpire!

903 **W**hy does someone who runs marathons make a good student?

Because education pays off in the long run!

904 **W**hat kind of sports stadium is always windy?

One filled with fans.

905 **W**hat stories do basketball players tell?

Tall tales!

906 **W**hat do Olympic sprinters eat before a race?
Nothing. They fast.

907 **W**hy do bowling pins have a tough time?
They always get knocked down.

908 **W**hat is a runner's favorite subject in school?
Jog-raphy!

Foolish Fun

909 **W**hy did the crazy sailor grab some soap when his ship sank?

Because he thought he would wash ashore.

910 **W**hy did the team of fools always lose the tug-of-war?

They pushed.

911   A crazy bank robber rushes into a bank, points two fingers at the teller and says, *"This is a muckup."*

"Don't you mean a stickup?" said the teller.

"No. It's a muckup," replied the robber. *"I've forgotten my gun!"*

912   The teacher told the fool she knew he'd skipped school last Friday, and heard he'd been playing games at the arcade.

The fool told her it wasn't true – and he had the baseball game tickets to prove it!

913   How does a fool call his dog?

He puts two fingers in his mouth and shouts "Rover!"

914   The fool saw a sign outside a police station that read *Man Wanted For Robbery*, and went in and applied for the job!

915 The gang's boss was surprised to find one of his gang sawing the legs off his bed.

"Why are you doing that?" he asked.

"Well, you did ask me to lie low for a bit," the fool replied.

916 Have you heard about the fool who thinks a fjord is a Scandinavian motor car?

917 Susie asked the fool if his tent leaked when he was on vacation.

"Only when it rained," he said.

918 **W**hy did the crazy pilot land his plane on a house?
Because the homeowner had left the landing lights on.

919 **H**ave you heard about the fool who went into a store open 24 hours and asked what time they closed?

What Do You Call...

920   ... a fairy who never takes a bath?

Stinkerbell!

921   ... a man with a paper bag on his head?

Russell!

922 ... a man with a seagull on his head?
Cliff!

923 ... a man with a map on his head?
Miles!

924 ... the chief's naughty daughter?
Miss Chief!

925 ... a woman with one leg?
Eileen!

926 ... a man with some cat scratches on his head?
Claude!

927 ... a man with a large black and blue mark on his head?

Bruce!

928 ... an egg laid by a dog?

A pooched egg!

929 ... a boy with an encyclopedia in his pants?

Smarty pants.

930 ... the hungry train?

It went chew chew!

931 ... a woman standing in a breeze?

Gail!

932   ... an elephant that flies?

A jumbo jet!

933   ... a woman with a tortoise on her head?

Shelley!

934   ... a cat that joined the Red Cross?

A first aid kit!

935   ... a pig that does karate?

Pork chop!

936   … a rabbit locked in a sauna?
A hot cross bunny!

937   … a man with a legal document?
Will!

938   … a man who shaves 15 times a day?
A barber!

939   … a deer with no eyes?
No idea!

940 ... a deer with no eyes and no legs?
Still no idea!

941 ... a messy cat?
Kitty Litterer!

942   ... a Russian fish?
Tsardine!

943   ... a pig with no clothes on?
Streaky bacon!

944   ... a well-behaved goose?
A propaganda!

945   ... a the ghost of a chicken?
A poultrygeist!

946 ... a bear with no fur?

A bare!

Sure it might be cool for a bear to shave all over and wear boxer shorts in Summer... But let's just hope his fur grows back by Winter!

Did You Hear About...

947 ... the girl who was so silly that when she ate M&Ms she threw out all the 'W's?

948 ... the man that was so ugly when he walked into the room, the mice jumped on chairs?

949 ... the man who took the mobile phone back to the store because it had no cord?

950 ... the girl who threw her guitar away because it had a hole in the middle?

951 ... the boy who ran so slowly he couldn't even catch his breath?

952 ... the pirate who was so silly he wore two eye patches?

953 ... the Italian chef?
He pasta way.

954 ... the fire at the circus?
It was in tents.

955 ... the girl with no left arm and no left leg?
She's all right.

956 ...the boy who was painting the fence?

The instructions said to put on three coats, so he put on his jacket, his parka and his raincoat.

957 ... the man who stole a bar of soap?
He made a clean getaway.

958 ... the silly sailor who was discharged from his submarine duties?
He was found sleeping with the window open.

959 ... the silly cyclist who won the Tour de France?
He did a lap of honor.

960 ... the foolish karate champion who joined the army?
The first time he saluted, he nearly killed himself.

961 ... the crazy hitchhiker?
He left home early so there wouldn't be much traffic.

962 ... the crazy photographer?

He saved used light bulbs for his dark room.

963 ... the fake noodle?

It was an impasta.

964 ... the claustrophobic astronaut?

He needed a little space.

965 ... the robber who stole a calendar?

He got 12 months

966 ... the Indian restaurant called Karma?

There's no menu; you just get what you deserve.

967 … the actress who fell through the floorboards?

She was just going through a stage.

968 … the sign at the music shop?

It said "Gone Chopin. Bach in a minute."

969 …the octopus couple who walked down the road?

They went arm in arm, in arm, in arm, in arm, in arm, in arm, in arm, in arm.

970 … the hen who counted her eggs?

She was a mathemachicken.

971 … the silly boy who stayed up all night to see where the sun went?

It finally dawned on him.

972 … the satellite dishes that got married?

The wedding was average but the reception was great!

973 … the tap dancer?

She fell into the sink.

TAP
TAP
TAP
BANG
THUMP

974 … the man who opened the flea circus?

He started it from scratch.

975 … the girl who drowned in a bowl of muesli?

A strong currant pulled her under.

976 ... the kidnapping in the park?
They woke him up.

977 ... the florist who had two kids?
One is a budding genius and the other is a blooming fool.

978 ... the musical ghost?
He wrote a haunting melody.

Wicked

979 "Daddy, can I have another glass of water, please?"
"Okay, but that's the twelfth one I've given you tonight."
"Yes I know, but my bedroom is still on fire."

980 John: *"Do you know anyone who has gone on the television?"*
Wendy: *"Just my dog, but he's housetrained now."*

981 Why are naughty kids like maggots?
Because they try to wriggle out of everything.

982 **D**id you hear about the two fat men who ran a marathon?

One ran in short bursts, the other ran in burst shorts.

983 **D**id you hear about the dentist who became a brain surgeon?

His drill slipped.

984 **A** woman woke her husband in the middle of the night.

"There's a burglar in the kitchen eating the cake I made!" she said.

"Who should I call?" asked her husband. "The police or an ambulance?"

985 **W**hat was proved when the steam roller ran over the man?

That he had lots of guts.

986 **D**id you hear about the two bodies cremated at the same time?

It was a dead heat.

The next scene is just too ugly to draw...!

987 **T**he cruise ship passenger was feeling really seasick, when the waiter asked if he'd like some lunch.

"No thanks," he replied. *"Just throw it over the side and save me the trouble."*

988 **W**hy did the tomato blush?

Because it saw the salad dressing.

989 **A** mushroom walks onto the playground and asks *"Can I play?"*

But the other kids refuse.

The mushroom says, *"Why not? I'm a fun-gi!"*

990 **A** man out for a walk came across a little boy pulling his cat's tail.

"Hey you!" he shouted. *"Don't pull the cat's tail!"*

"I'm not pulling," replied the boy. *"I'm only holding on. The cat's doing the pulling!"*

991 **H**airdresser: "Would you like a haircut?"

Boy: *"No, I'd like them all cut."*

992 **T**hree guys, Shutup, Manners, and Poop, were walking down the road when Poop fell down. Shutup went to get help. He found a policeman who asked, *"What's your name?"*

"Shutup," he answered.

"Hey, where are your manners!" the policeman exclaimed.

Shutup replied, *"Outside on the road, picking up Poop!"*

993 **F**ather: *"Johnny got an A on his assignment! I think he got his brains from me."*

Mother: *"I think you're right. I've still got mine."*

994 Sam: *"Mom, can I have a pony for Christmas?"*

Mom: *"Of course not. You'll have turkey just like the rest of us."*

995 Davey: *"Dad, there's a man at the door collecting for a new swimming pool."*

Dad: *"Alright, give him a glass of water."*

996 Have you ever seen a man-eating tiger?

No, but in a restaurant I once saw a man eating chicken.

997 **W**hat do you get when an elephant stands on your roof?

Mushed rooms.

998 **W**hat did the dragon say when he saw the knight in his shining armor?

"Oh no! Not more canned food!"

999 **W**hat goes in many different colors but always comes out blue?

A swimmer on a cold day!

1000 **W**here would you get a job playing an elastic trumpet?

In a rubber band!

1001 Why does the ocean roar?

Because there are crabs on its bottom.